Kermit
Learns
How Computers Work

Starring Jim Henson's Muppets™

by Margy Kuntz
Illustrations by Tom Brannon
Computer color by Tasa Graphic Arts, Inc.

P PRIMA

Muppet Press

Oh boy! Am I glad to see you! I just got the most exciting thing, and I've been waiting to show it to you!

Isn't it wonderful? My brand-new computer! I can't wait to try it out!

Just think of all the things I can do with this.
I can write great plays for Piggy . . .

paint pictures of my friends . . .

play songs with Rowlf . . .

I can even become the world's best airplane pilot!

Sheesh. Maybe I'm getting a little carried away. See, I know the computer isn't a magician. It can't turn me into something I'm not. But it *can* make the things I do easier or faster or more fun.

And I'll tell you something else I just found out. Computers can't think for themselves! Yup, it's true. They can *follow* orders, but they can't think them up.

You probably know that these are computer disks. They help make the computer seem so smart. But did you know a disk has a special set of instructions on it called a **program**? The program tells the computer exactly what to do.

A program is like a recipe. It tells the computer how to "mix" different pieces of information together. For instance, say the computer needed to subtract the number 2 from the number 4. The program would tell it to take the number 4 and then subtract the number 2 from it. Without the program, the computer might subtract 4 from 2 instead of 2 from 4. It might even use the wrong numbers!

And do you know why you can do so many
different things on a computer? Because every
program is a different "recipe," or set of orders!
Some programs tell the computer how to draw
pictures. Others tell it how to form words. Some
help it make the sounds you hear, and some tell
it how to do math.

But even though programs tell the computer *how* to do things, the computer still needs to know what ingredients to work with. And guess who gives the computer the ingredients to use? *You* do!

Let's say you type the word *MOM* on your **keyboard**. Each time you press a key, the keyboard sends a message to the computer. The M key says, "I want an *M*," the O key says, "I want an *O*," and the M key says, "I want an *M* again." *M* and *O* are the ingredients for the word *MOM*.

The keyboard is one way you can send
messages to your computer, but it's not the
only way. Here's something else you can use.
It's called a **mouse**. (This isn't an animal
mouse, of course; it's a computer mouse!)

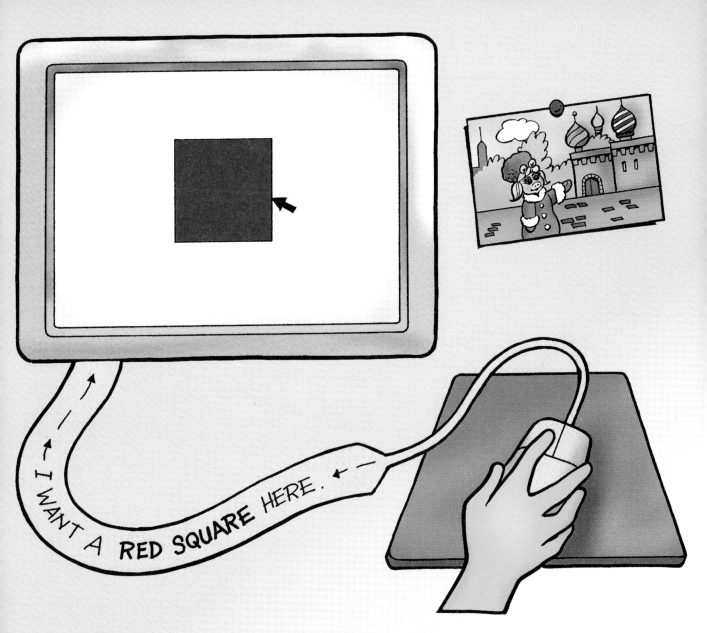

When you move the mouse, or click on the buttons on top, it sends messages to the computer, just as the keyboard does. You can use it to move things on the screen or to say such things as, "I want a green, straight line here" or "I want a red square here."

A **joystick** is another way of sending messages to the computer. When you play games, the joystick lets you go up, down, left, or right.

All of the messages you send to the computer are called **input** because you are putting them into the computer. Get it? Put in, input! The messages that go out from the computer to the screen or to the printer are called output because they are put out by the computer.

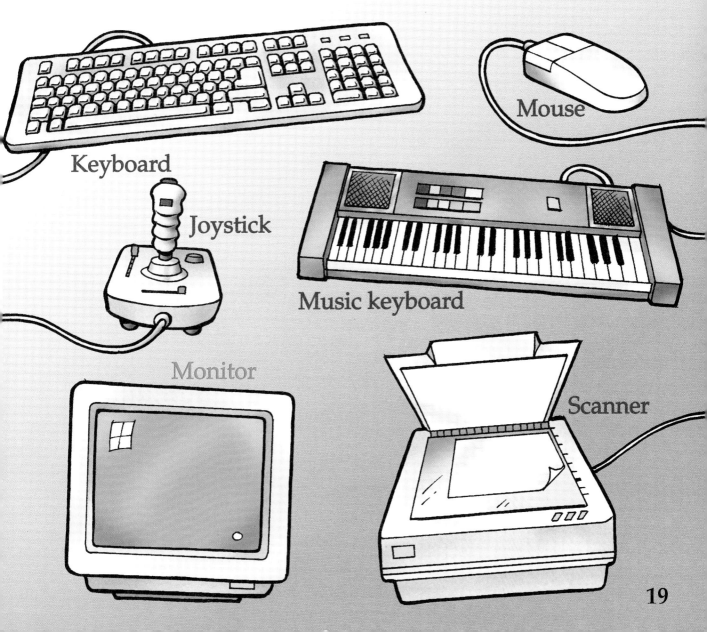

Keyboard

Mouse

Joystick

Music keyboard

Monitor

Scanner

19

Now, when I found out that the computer gets all these messages and instructions all the time, I was a bit worried! I mean, how does it keep everything straight?

But Scooter told me I shouldn't worry. He said that inside the computer is something that helps the computer know what to do. It's the computer's brain.

Of course, a computer's brain isn't like ours. In some computers, it's very, very small—no bigger than a baby's fingernail. People who work with computers a lot call it the **CPU**, or **central processing unit**. And it's made of a material called silicon.

Imagine that we could be small enough to take a walk inside a computer. Then we could really see how it works!

Of course, you should never open a computer or anything else with electricity in it.

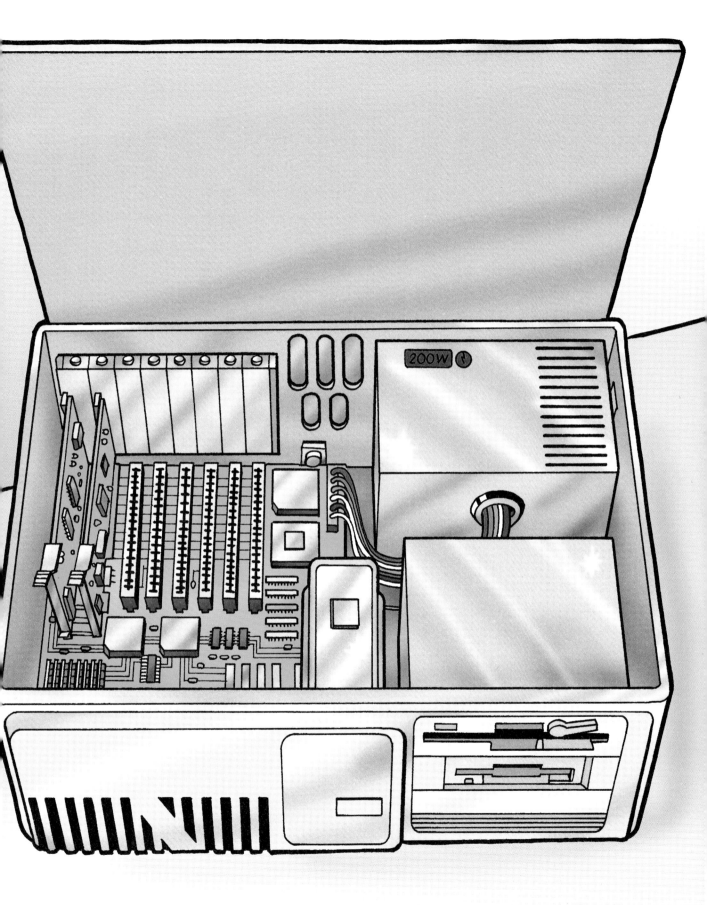

Isn't the view great from up here? It sort of looks like a giant city, doesn't it? (Your computer might not look exactly like this, but all computers have basically the same parts.)

In fact, the computer sort of works like a city, too. All the messages rush around from place to place, like cars on roads. And the computer's CPU, its brain, directs the traffic. It tells some cars they can move, makes others wait, and gives directions about how to get from place to place.

Speaking of cars and roads, I bet you're wondering about all these things that look like roads. They're really wires and metal pieces. In fact, some of the "roads" are really the size of a human hair. Pretty amazing, huh? They're what carry messages around to different parts of the computer.

These things that look like buildings are the different parts of the computer. Each one does a different job.

And here's the CPU — the computer's brain!
Well, actually, . . . it's just the covering. Inside
the covering is the brain itself.

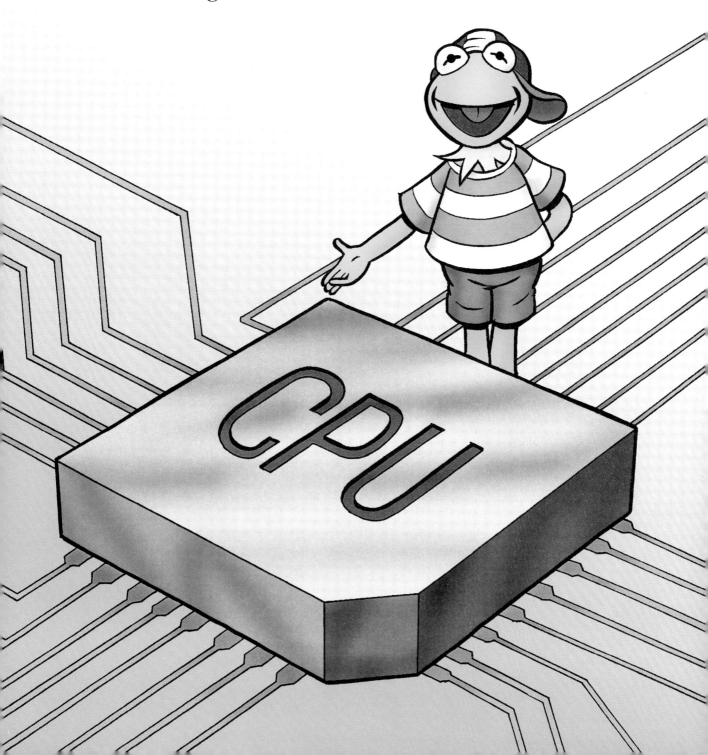

The CPU has a lot of work to do. It makes sure the program's instructions are carried out. First, it reads each line of the program's orders. Then it sends a message to another part of the computer, telling it what to do. Of course, the computer reads and sends messages much more quickly than we can.

I NEED A "4"

I NEED A "+"

RE IS AN "O"

HERE IS AN "M"

I NEED A SQUARE

I NEED RED

EED BLUE

I NEED A CIRCLE

I NEED

HERE IS A

HERE IS AN "E"

NEED A "5"

But even though the computer works very, very fast, it can only do one thing at a time. So it needs a place to put all its instructions and input until it has to have them. That place is called **memory**.

Everything is sorted out in the computer's memory, kind of like the way you keep your socks in one drawer and your shirts in another. Then when the program says something like, "Get an *E*," the CPU sends a message to the memory, saying, "Give me an *E*."

Everything your computer knows is kept in its memory. There are different kinds of memory. One is called **ROM**. Without ROM, your computer wouldn't even know what to do when you turn it on.

Then there's **RAM**. You can think of RAM as a table in the school library. When you want to work on a project, the librarian brings your books, pencils, notebook—all the things you need—so you can use them at the table. RAM does the same thing inside the computer. If you want to write a letter or draw a picture, the CPU brings everything you need to RAM. It holds everything you are working on there.

When your work is done in the library, you must put all of your things away or else you might lose them. You also have to put your things away when you are using the computer. It's called saving your work. Do you know why? Because if you turn off the computer without saving your work . . . poof! It will all disappear. RAM doesn't remember anything when you turn the computer off.

That's why you need one more kind of memory — the kind you keep on disks. Your computer may have a **hard disk** hidden inside it. It may also have openings for **floppy disks**. Either way, the disks are where you keep things that you want the computer to remember and show you later.

WELCOME
TO THE
COMPUTER
INFORMATION
ROOM

CPU
LIBRARIAN

So let's say you want to write a note to a friend, using the computer. You turn the computer on, and then you start up a writing program from either the hard disk or a floppy disk by sending it to RAM — the work area. When you use the computer's keyboard to type your note, it sends messages to the CPU, saying things like, "I want a *D*, then an *E*, then an *A*, and then an *R*."

The CPU, the computer's brain, reads the messages one at a time and sends them off to RAM. The letters—D, E, A, R—then appear on the computer screen in your writing program.

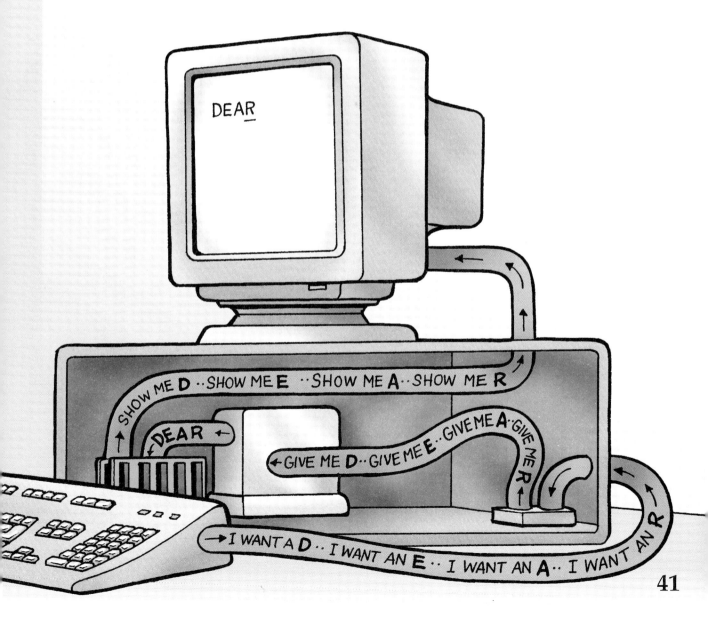

You can also tell the computer you want the letters sent to a **printer**, so you can give the note to your friend.

That's how the computer helps you write
letters to your friends. You can also paint
pictures, play games, tell the time, and do lots
of other great stuff with your computer.

So now that you know the sorts of things a computer can help you do . . . what would *you* like to do?

Words to Know

CPU (central processing unit): The computer's brain. It reads the messages you send it and tells the other parts of the computer what to do.

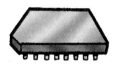

Floppy disk: Often it's hard and square, so why do they call it a floppy disk? Because a thin, floppy disk is *inside* the hard plastic covering! You save things on a floppy disk, just as you would record your favorite songs on a cassette tape.

Hard disk: The big disk inside your computer. You can keep lots more stuff on it than you can on a floppy disk. The hard disk is where you usually store the programs you use on your computer.

Hardware: This is all the stuff that sits on your desk, including the keyboard, monitor, mouse, printer, and so on. Hardware isn't any good without *software*. The programs that make your computer run and let you do fun things with it are called software.

Input: What you tell your computer to do. You can use a joystick, a keyboard, or a mouse to send messages (input) to your computer. Your computer doesn't know what to do until *you* give it instructions.

Joystick: You use this when you're playing games. It sends messages to the computer that make you go left, right, up, and down.

Keyboard: This sits in front of your computer and lets you send messages  to make numbers and letters and special symbols (like $, &, and *). The keyboard also has keys that let you move around on the screen and do other things, too.

Memory: The computer remembers things, just as you do! It uses the hard disk to keep things it has to remember for a long time. There are two other kinds of memory as well: RAM and ROM.

Monitor: The part of your computer that shows you words and pictures. It looks sort of like a little television sitting behind your keyboard.

Mouse: The thing that's shaped like a bar of soap with a marble under it. When you move it around and click on its buttons, it sends messages (input) to your computer.

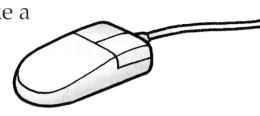

Output: When you send messages to your computer (see **Input**), it takes that information and sends it to the screen (monitor) or to a printer so you can see what it has done. This is output.

Printer: A machine that takes the words and pictures you have created on your computer and puts them onto the paper.

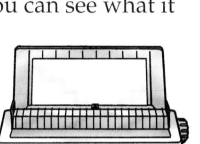

Program: A big recipe (or set of rules) that tells your computer how to create words and numbers, show pictures, or play games. Without a program, your computer wouldn't be able to understand anything you told it. Programs are also called *software*.

RAM (random-access memory): The place where the computer keeps the things you are working on. If you are writing a letter to a friend on your computer, it keeps the letter in RAM until you save it onto a disk. When you turn the computer off, it forgets everything in RAM. (So don't forget to save your work!)

ROM (read-only memory): This part of memory is always there, whether the computer is on or off. It tells the computer the most basic things it needs to know just to get started.

Zorxyl: There really isn't anything in a computer called a zorxyl, but everybody knows you have to end a word list with "Z"!